AF426029

Cataraqui United Church Cemetery 2

The Grave Whisperer

Angeline Gallant

Published by Angeline Gallant, 2022.

While every precaution has been taken in the preparation of this book, the publisher assumes no responsibility for errors or omissions, or for damages resulting from the use of the information contained herein.

CATARAQUI UNITED CHURCH CEMETERY 2

First edition. October 1, 2022.

Copyright © 2022 Angeline Gallant.

ISBN: 979-8215734339

Written by Angeline Gallant.

Also by Angeline Gallant

Calling Her Heart
Whisper of the Heart
No Turning Back
Forsake Me Not
Hear My Cry

Keeper Of Secrets
A Lady's Secret

Midnight's Awakening
Heart of the Storm
Walking Through The Storm

Secrets of the Underworld
Deklan's Dragons

Tell My Story Collection

Tell My Story: England 1852

The Grave Whisperer
Wedding Bells in Kingston, Ontario, Canada 1923
St. Paul's Anglican Churchyard Kingston, Ontario, Canada A-B
St. Paul's Anglican Churchyard, Kingston, Ontario, Canada C - D
St. Paul's Anglican Churchyard, Kingston, Ontario, Canada G - H
St. Paul's Anglican Churchyard, Kingston, Ontario, Canada J - N
St. Paul's Anglican Churchyard, Kingston, Ontario, Canada O - R
St. Paul's Anglican Churchyard, Kingston, Ontario, Canada S - T
St. Paul's Anglican Churchyard, Kingston, Ontario T - Z
Small Graveyards & Burial Grounds: Kingston, Ontario, Canada
Cataraqui United Church Cemetery 1
Cataraqui United Church Cemetery 2

The Wolf Whisperer Series
The Cry of the Wolf
Captured Heart
Journey of the Heart
Fate's Legacy
Wolf Whisperer volumes 1 & 2
Endless White

Standalone
Winds of Change vol 1-3

Watch for more at https://www.goodreads.com/author/show/19703964.Angeline_Gallant.

Table of Contents

ALBERTA EVELINIA "BERTIE" BENJAMIN[1]

Bertie was born on August 8, 1870 in Camden East, Ontario.

She was not yet a year old when British Columbia joined the confederation in 1871.

Bertie was 12 years old when the mining boom in northern Ontario began in 1883.

She was 19 years old when her mother passed away in 1890.

Bertie was 20 years old when she passed away on June 20, 1891 in Camden East. She is buried in Kingston, Ontario.

AMELIA (MILLER) BENJAMIN[2]

Amelia was born in 1840.

She was 25 years old when she married Isaac Benjamin on December 25, 1864 in Ernestown, Ontario.

Amelia was 27 years old when Ontario was founded on July 1, 1867.

She was 28 years old when her firstborn, Henry Overton, passed away in 1868. He was only three years old.

Amelia was 31 years old when British Columbia joined the confederation in 1871.

She was 43 years old when the mining boom in northern Ontario began in 1883.

Amelia was 53 years old when her sister, Martha Ann, passed away in 1890. She passed away on June 11th in the same year as her sister.

EBENEZER BENJAMIN[3]

Ebenezer was born in Upper Canada in 1820.

He was 47 years old when Ontario was founded on July 1, 1867.

Ebenezer was 51 years old when British Columbia joined the confederation in 1871.

He was 63 years old when his daughter, Elizabeth Ann, passed away in 1883.

Ebenezer was 69 years old when he passed away in 1889.

HENRY OVERTON BENJAMIN[4]

Henry was born in 1865.

He was two years old when Ontario was founded on July 1, 1867.

Henry was three years old when he passed away on August 1, 1868.

MARIA (CATON) BENJAMIN[5]

Maria was born in Ernestown in 1818.

She was 16 years old when her mother passed away in 1834.

Maria was 20 years old when her father passed away in 1838.

She was 27 years old when her sister Harriet passed away in 1845.

Maria was 49 years old when Ontario was founded on July 1, 1867.

She was 53 years old when British Columbia joined the confederation in 1871.

Maria was 65 years old when her daughter, Eliza Ann, passed away in 1883.

She was 71 years old when her husband passed away in 1889.

Maria was 78 years old when she passed away on June 6, 1896.

SAMUEL BENJAMIN[6]

Samuel was born in Ernestown in 1839.

He was 21 years old when his sister, Mary Miranda, passed away on December 3, 1860.

Samuel was 23 years old when he passed away on May 16, 1862.

EARL EDGAR BENNINGTON[7]

Earl passed away on March 1, 1910 in Washington, USA. He is buried in Kingston, Ontario.

WILLIAM TOBIAS BEVENS[8]

William was born in Lyndhurst, Ontario in 1921.

He was 13 years old when the Dionne Quintuplets were born in 1934.

William was 39 years old when his mother passed away in 1960.

He was 61 years old when the Canada Act was passed in 1982.

William was 76 years old when his wife, Lillian Easter, passed away in 1997.

He was 81 years old when his brother, Garfield Hilliard, passed away in 2002.

William was 84 years old when his sister, Dorothy Irene, passed away in 2005.

He was 85 years old when he passed away on December 19, 2005.

HENRY SHAYLER BICKNELL[9]

Henry was born on September 28, 1841.
He was 53 years old when he passed away on May 3, 1895.

IDA AMELIA (WARTMAN) BICKNELL[10]

Ida was born in 1863.

She was four years old when Ontario was established on July 1, 1867.

Ida was eight years old when British Columbia joined the confederation in 1871.

She was 20 years old when the mining boom in northern Ontario began in 1883.

Ida was 29 years old when she married Henry Bicknell on April 27, 1892 in Frontenac, Ontario.

She was 32 years old when her first child, Jennie, who was only 11 months old, passed away on April 12, 1895. Her husband passed away on May 3rd.

Ida was 40 years old when her mother passed away in 1903.

She was 43 years old when Ontario Hydro was established in 1906.

Ida was 45 years old when her father passed away in 1908.

She was 48 years old when her brother, John Alfred, passed away in 1911.

Ida was 59 years old when her brother, Charles Henry, passed away in 1922.

She was 62 years old when her brother, Sherman Everitt, passed away in 1925.

Ida was 64 years old when her sister, Agnes Evaline Adelaide, passed away in 1927.

She was 71 years old when the Dionne Quintuplets were born in 1934.

Ida was 78 years old when she passed away in 1941.

JENNIE BICKNELL[11]

Jennie was born in Napanee, Ontario on March 7, 1894. She was a year old when she passed away on April 12, 1895.

D. PEARL (SMITH) BLUNDELL[12]

Pearl was born in 1919.

She was 15 years old when the Dionne Quintuplets were born in 1934.

Pearl was 63 years old when the Canada Act was passed in 1982.

She was 72 years old when she passed away in 1991.

WILLIAM HENRY BLUNDELL[13]

William was born in 1908.

He was 26 years old when the Dionne Quintuplets were born in 1934.

William was 74 years old when the Canada Act was passed in 1982.

He was 79 years old when he passed away in 1987.

JOSHUA BOOTH[14]

Joshua passed away on November 25, 1864 in Kingston, Frontenac, Canada West, British Colonial America.

MARY ELLEN BOOTH[15]

Mary passed away on November 24, 1864, a day before her husband, Joshua Booth.

THOMAS BRADLEY[16]

Thomas passed away on April 24, 1849.

WALLACE G. R. BRIDGE[17]

Wallace was born in 1860.

He was seven years old when Ontario was founded on July 1, 1867.

Wallace was eight years old when his mother passed away on August 23, 1868. His brother, William Richard, passed away a few days later on August 30th.

He was 11 years old when British Columbia joined the confederation in 1871.

Wallace was 22 years old when his brother, Charles Henry, passed away in 1882.

He was 23 years old when the mining boom in northern Ontario began in 1883.

Wallace was 25 years old when he married Margaret Geagh on April 21, 1885.

He was 32 years old when his sister, Mary Elizabeth, passed away in 1892.

Wallace was 38 years old when he passed away on April 12, 1898.

DUANE CLARK BRONSON[18]

Duane was born in 1918 in Cornwall, Ontario.

He was 15 years old when the Dionne Quintuplets were born in 1934.

Duane was 34 years old when his mother passed away in 1953.

He was 38 years old when his sister, Winnifred May, passed away in 1957.

Duane was 44 years old when his father passed away in 1962.

He was 52 years old when his brother, Nathan Stuart, passed away in 1971.

Duane was 67 years old when his brother, Otis Seaton, passed away in 1986.

He was 81 years old when he passed away in 2000.

EVEYLYN A. (HARTLE) BRONSON[19]

Evelyn was born in 1919.

She was 16 years old when the Dionne Quintuplets were born in 1934.

Evelyn was 64 years old when the Canada Act was passed in 1982.

She was 81 years old when she passed away in 1999.

WALTER BRONSON[20]

Walter was born in 1817.

He was 50 years old when Ontario was founded on July 1, 1867.

Walter was 54 years old when he passed away on June 1, 1871.

THOMAS BROWN[21]

Thomas was born in 1838.

He was 29 years old when Ontario was founded on July 1, 1867.

Thomas was 33 years old when British Columbia joined the confederation in 1871.

He was 78 years old when he passed away in 1916.

ISABELLA CATHERINE (TAYLOR) BULCH[22]

Isabella was born on November 26, 1829 in Westbrook, Ontario. She was Dutch.

She was 37 years old when Ontario was founded on July 1, 1867.

Isabella was 41 years old when her husband, Christopher John Bulch, passed away in 1870.

She was 53 years old when the mining boom in northern Ontario began in 1883.

Isabella was 86 years old when her daughter, Sarah, passed away in 1916.

She was 87 years old when WWI began in 1917.

Isabella was 91 years old when her son, Joseph, passed away in 1920.

She was 92 years old when she passed away in 1922. Isabella was Methodist.

A. ETHEL (BULLOCK) GLOVER[23]

Ethel was born in 1883, the same year that there was a mining boom in northern Ontario.

She was 66 years old when she passed away in 1949.

EDWARD BULLOCK[24]

Edward was born in 1916.

He was four years old when his father passed away in 1920.

Edward was 17 years old when the Dionne Quintuplets were born in 1934.

He was 64 years old when he passed away in 1980.

GWENDOLYN (SMITH) BULLOCK[25]

Gwendolyn was born in 1922.

She was 12 years old when the Dionne Quintuplets were born in 1934.

Gwendolyn was 59 years old when her husband passed away in 1980.

She was 60 years old when the Canada Act was passed in 1982.

Gwendolyn was 80 years old when she passed away in 2002.

GEORGE NORMAN "NORM" BUNKER[26]

George was born on May 14, 1892.

Between 1901 - 1911 he was Methodist and living in Simcoe, Ontario.

He was 13 years old when Ontario Hydro was established in 1906.

Norm was 26 years old when he married Vida Amelia Smythe on May 25, 1918 in Kingston, Ontario.

He was 41 years old when the Dionne Quintuplets were born in 1934.

Norm was 42 years old when his father passed away in 1934.

He was 49 years old when his mother passed away in 1941.

Norm was 54 years old when his sister, Estella Louisa, passed away in 1946.

He was 62 years old when he passed away in 1955.

VIDA AMELIA (SMYTHE) BUNKER[27]

Vida was born on February 18, 1894 in Gananoque, Ontario. She was Dutch.

She was seven years old when her sister, Robyn, passed away in 1901.

Vida was 11 years old when Ontario Hydro was established in 1906.

She was 24 years old when she married George Norman Bunker on May 25, 1918 in Kingston.

Vida was 26 years old when her mother passed away in 1921.

She was 39 years old when the Dionne Quintuplets were born in 1934.

Vida was 46 years old when her father passed away in 1940.

She was 61 years old when her husband passed away in 1955.

Vida was 87 years old when the Canada Act was passed in 1982.

She was 94 years old when she passed away in 1988. Vida was Methodist.

NANCY (MYERS) BURDETT[28]

Nancy was born in 1760.
She was 43 years old when she passed away in 1903.

REV. ADAM HOOD BURWELL[29]

Adam was born in 1790.

He was 34 years old when the Crimes Act was passed in 1825.

Adam was 35 years old when his mother passed away in 1825.

He was 38 years old when his father passed away in 1838.

Adam was 55 years old when his brother, Mahlon, passed away in 1846.

He was 59 years old when he passed away in 1849. Adam was a pastor, journalist and writer.

JAMES BUTLAND[30]

James was born in 1869 in Torquay, Devon, England.

He was two years old when British Columbia joined the confederation in 1871.

James was 14 years old when the mining boom began in northern Ontario in 1883.

He was 28 years old when he passed away in 1897.

MARGARET HAY (BUTLAND) BELL[31]

Margaret was born in 1873.

She was 10 years old when the mining boom in northern Ontario began in 1883.

Margaret was 78 years old when she passed away in 1951.

ANNIE (CROSS) CAIRNS[32]

Annie was born on August 29, 1859 in Wiltshire, England. She was Irish.

She was 26 years old when she married William Charles Cairns on August 1, 1886 in Panteg, Wales.

Annie was 33 years old when her son, Walter Frank, passed away in 1893.

She was 36 years old when her son, George Ivor Patrick, passed away in 1896 when he was only ten months old.

Annie was 41 years old when her four-year-old son, Francis Ivor Howard, passed away in 1900.

She immigrated to Canada in 1905.

Annie was 46 years old when Ontario Hydro was established in 1906.

She was 51 years old and living in Wentworth, Ontario in 1911.

Annie was 54 years old when Britain entered into The Great War in 1914.

She was 58 years old when her son, Charles Ridley, was killed in Vimy, France in 1917.

Annie was 59 years old when her son, William John, was killed in Vimy, France in 1918.

She was 63 years old when her son, Albert Reginald Sidney, passed away in 1923.

Annie was 66 years old when her husband passed away in 1925. Her daughter, Beatrice Kathleen, passed away in 1926.

She was 71 years old when she passed away on May 31, 1931 in Toronto, Ontario. Annie was Anglican.

WILLIAM CHARLES CAIRNS[33]

William was born in Ireland in 1857.

He was 29 years old when he married Annie Cross on August 1, 1886 in Panteg, Wales.

He was 33 years old and living in Penarth, Wales as a domestic servant in 1891.

William was 35 years old when his son, Walter Frank, passed away in 1893.

He was 39 years old when his son, George Ivor Patrick, passed away in 1896.

William was 43 years old when his son, Francis Ivor Howard, passed away in 1900.

He was 44 years old and working as a gardener in 1901.

William was 53 years old when he lived in Wentworth, Ontario in 1911. He was Anglican.

He was 60 years old when his son, Charles Ridley, died at Vimy, France in 1917.

William was 61 years old when his son, William John, died at Vimy, France in 1918.

He was 65 years old when his son, Albert Reginald Sidney, passed away in 1923.

William was 68 years old when he passed away on October 8, 1925.

ARCHIBALD WADDELL CAMPBELL[34]

Archibald was born on October 28, 1874 in Calton, Glasgow, Scotland.

He was three years old when the collapse of the Glasgow bank took place in 1878.

Archibald was 16 years old in 1891 and living in Shettleston, Scotland where he was working as a railway porter.

He was 38 years old when he married Hannah Rose Main on June 5, 1913 in Kingston, Ontario. She was 50 years old.

Archibald was 54 years old when his wife passed away in 1929.

He was 78 years old when Queen Elizabeth II was crowned in 1953.

Archibald was 90 years old when he passed away in 1965. He was a Christian.

MYRTLE M. (CARPENTER) HOGAN[35]

Myrtle was born in 1883, the same year that the mining boom in northern Ontario began.

She was 23 years old when Ontario Hydro was established in 1907.

Myrtle was 47 years old when she passed away in 1930.

RODERICK CRYSLER CARTER[36]

Roderick was born on December 5, 1843.

He was 23 years old when Ontario was founded on July 1, 1867.

Rockerick was 37 years old and working as a lumberman merchant in 1881.

He was 39 years old when the mining boom in northern Ontario began in 1883.

Roderick was 57 years old and living in Montreal, Quebec in 1901.

He was 77 years old when he passed away on February 28, 1921.

VERNA EDITH (SCOTT) CARTER[37]

Verna was born on January 16, 1915.

She was 18 years old when the Dionne Quintuplets were born in 1934.

Verna was 67 years old when the Canada Act was passed in 1982.

She was 101 years old when she passed away on June 8, 2016 in Selby, Ontario. Verna is buried in Kingston, Ontario.

EDWIN WILLIAM "WILLIAM" CAVANAGH[38]

William was born in England in 1891.

He was 13 years old when the Entente Codiale was signed in 1904.

William was 27 years old when he married Florence Mildred Vanluven on September 16, 1924 in Kingston, Ontario.

He was 62 years old when Queen Elizabeth II was crowned in 1953.

William was 76 years old when he passed away in 1967.

FLORENCE MILDREN (VanLUVEN) CAVANAGH[39]

Florence was born in New York in 1904.

She was living in Lyme, Jefferson, New York when she was a year old.

Florence was four years old when the Bureau of Investigation was formed in 1908.

She was six years old when the Mann Act was passed in 1910.

Florence was 20 years old when she married Edwin William Cavanagh on September 16, 1924 in Kingston, Ontario.

She was 34 years old when the Dionne Quintuplets were born in 1934.

Florence was 38 years old when her brother, Robert, passed away in 1942.

She was 39 years old when her father passed away in 1943.

Florence was 63 years old when her husband passed away in 1967.

She was 72 years old when she passed away in 1976.

PVT. JOHN M. CAVANAGH[40]

John was 68 years old when he passed away on April 14, 1995. He was in the R. C. O. C.

ROYDEN CAVANAGH[41]

Royden was born in 1939.

He was 17 years old when he passed away in 1956. It is said that he was accidentally poisoned by oil of wintergreen.

NATHANIEL CAVERLEY[42]

Nathaniel was 83 years old when he passed away on August 18, 1854.

EMILY LOUISA HENRIETTA CAVERLEY[43]

Emily was born in 1870. She was German.

She was a year old when British Columbia joined the confederation in 1871.

Emily was 13 years old when the mining boom in northern Ontario began in 1883.

She was 19 years old when her father passed away in 1889.

Emily was 36 years old when Ontario Hydro was established in 1906.

She was 43 years old when her mother passed away in 1913.

Emily was 45 years old when she passed away on March 26, 1915.

EMILY VICTORIA CAVERLEY[44]

Emily was born in 1849.

She was 17 years old when she passed away on January 2, 1867.

MARGARET (HORNING) CAVERLEY[45]

Margaret was born on January 11, 1807. She was German. She was 44 years old when her sister, Lena, passed away in 1851.

Margaret was 49 years old when her mother passed away in 1856.

She was 52 years old when her father passed away on April 6, 1859. Her sister, Catherine, passed away on May 13th.

Margaret was 60 years old when her daughter, Emiliy Victoria, passed away in 1867.

She was 64 years old when British Columbia joined the confederation in 1871. Margaret was Methodist and living in Storrington, Ontario at that time.

Margaret was 71 years old when her husband passed away in 1878.

She was 81 years old when she passed away on August 2, 1888 in Storrington, Ontario. Margaret is buried in Kingston, Ontario.

MELISSA JANE CAVERLEY[46]

Melissa was born in 1847.

She was 19 years old when she passed away on December 21, 1866.

PHOEBE ANN (WRIGHT) CAVERLY[47]

Phoebe was born on January 22, 1838 in Sidney, Ontario.

She was 12 years old when her brother, Alexander, passed away in 1850.

Phoebe was 22 years old when she married William Caverly on April 24, 1860 in Frontenac, Ontario.

She was 27 years when her sister, Margaret Elizabeth, passed away in 1865.

Phoebe was 32 years old when British Columbia joined the confederation in 1871.

She was 51 years old when her husband passed away in 1889.

Phoebe was 57 years old when her father passed away in 1895. He was a pastor.

She was 58 years old when her mother passed away in 1896.

Phoebe was 67 years old when Ontario Hydro was established in 1906.

She was 68 years old when her brother, William John, passed away in 1906.

Phoebe was 75 years old when her sister, Frances Arvilla, passed away on April 13, 1913. She passed away on May 12th. Phoebe was German/ Irish and Methodist.

WILLIAM "RED BILLY" CAVERLY[48]

William was born on November 20, 1807 in Storrington, Frontenac, Upper Canada, British Colonial America. He was Scottish.

He was less than a year old when the Atlantic slave trade was abolished in 1808.

William was 21 years old when he married Margaret Horning on March 31, 1829.

He was 25 years old when his sister, Sarah Rosetta, passed away in 1833.

William was 42 years old when his father passed away in 1850.

He was 45 years old when his mother passed away in 1853.

William was 59 years old when his daughter, Melissa Jane, passed away in 1866.

He was 59 years old when his daughter, Emily Victoria, passed away in 1867.

William was 69 years old when his brother, John, passed away in 1877.

He was 71 years old when he passed away on November 12, 1878. William was Methodist.

WILLIAM CAVERLY[49]

William was born on February 9, 1836 in Storrington, Ontario. He was German/Irish.

He was 24 years old when he married Phoebe Ann Wright on April 24, 1860 in Frontenac, Ontario.

William was 30 years old when his sister Melissa Jane passed away on December 21, 1866. His sister, Emily Victoria, passed away on January 2, 1867.

He was 34 years old when British Columbia joined the confederation in 1871.

William was 42 years old when his father, William "Red Billy," passed away in 1878.

He was 46 years old when the mining boom in northern Ontario began in 1883.

William was 52 years old when he passed away on December 15, 1889 in Storrington, Ontario. He passed away in Kingston, Ontario. He was Methodist and a farmer.

LYDIA (BLOEMER) CAVRELY[50]

Lydia was 70 years old when she passed away on April 11, 1853.

ALLAN CHADWICK[51]

Allan was born in 1852.

He was 15 years old when Ontario was founded on July 1, 1867.

Allan was 19 years old when British Columbia joined the confederation in 1871.

He was 85 years old when he passed away in 1937.

WILLIAM MILES CHADWICK[52]

William was born in 1837.

He was 30 years old when Ontario was founded on July 1, 1867.

William was 34 years old when British Columbia joined the confederation in 1871.

He was 39 years old when his mother passed away in 1876.

William was 42 years old when he married Alice Jane Ashley on December 3, 1879 in Kingston, Ontario.

He was 45 years old when his sister, Eliza Jane, passed away in 1882.

William was 46 years old when the mining boom in northern Ontario began in 1883.

He was 59 years old when he passed away on February 5, 1896.

[1] https://www.wikitree.com/genealogy/Benjamin-Family-Tree-4075

[2] https://www.wikitree.com/genealogy/Miller-Family-Tree-101444

[3] https://www.wikitree.com/genealogy/Benjamin-Family-Tree-4076

[4] https://www.wikitree.com/genealogy/Benjamin-Family-Tree-4077

[5] https://www.wikitree.com/genealogy/Caton-Family-Tree-1272

[6] https://www.wikitree.com/genealogy/Benjamin-Family-Tree-3095

[7] https://www.wikitree.com/genealogy/Bennington-Family-Tree-623

[8] https://www.wikitree.com/genealogy/Bevens-Family-Tree-102

[9] https://www.wikitree.com/genealogy/Bicknell-Family-Tree-1395

[10] https://www.wikitree.com/genealogy/Wartman-Family-Tree-79

[11] https://www.wikitree.com/genealogy/Bicknell-Family-Tree-1396

[12] https://www.wikitree.com/genealogy/Smith-Family-Tree-286649

[13] https://www.wikitree.com/genealogy/Blundell-Family-Tree-1522

[14] https://www.wikitree.com/genealogy/Booth-Family-Tree-11233

[15] https://www.wikitree.com/genealogy/Unknown-Family-Tree-620092

[16] https://www.wikitree.com/genealogy/Bradley-Family-Tree-17722

[17] https://www.wikitree.com/genealogy/Bridge-Family-Tree-2455

[18] https://www.wikitree.com/genealogy/Bronson-Family-Tree-1810

[19] https://www.wikitree.com/genealogy/Hartle-Family-Tree-374

[20] https://www.wikitree.com/genealogy/Bronson-Family-Tree-1811

[21] https://www.wikitree.com/genealogy/Brown-Family-Tree-148195

[22] https://www.wikitree.com/genealogy/Taylor-Family-Tree-65813

[23] https://www.wikitree.com/genealogy/Bullock-Family-Tree-6374

[24] https://www.wikitree.com/genealogy/Bullock-Family-Tree-6375

[25] https://www.wikitree.com/genealogy/Smith-Family-Tree-286695

[26] https://www.wikitree.com/genealogy/Bunker-Family-Tree-2810

[27] https://www.wikitree.com/genealogy/Smythe-Family-Tree-1368

[28] https://www.wikitree.com/genealogy/Myers-Family-Tree-21901

[29] https://www.wikitree.com/genealogy/Burwell-Family-Tree-458

[30] https://www.wikitree.com/genealogy/Butland-Family-Tree-114

[31] https://www.wikitree.com/genealogy/Butland-Family-Tree-115

[32] https://www.wikitree.com/genealogy/Cross-Family-Tree-12804

[33] https://www.wikitree.com/genealogy/Cairns-Family-Tree-2119

[34] https://www.wikitree.com/genealogy/Campbell-Family-Tree-54553

[35] https://www.wikitree.com/genealogy/Carpenter-Family-Tree-23155

[36] https://www.wikitree.com/genealogy/Carter-Family-Tree-43503

[37] https://www.wikitree.com/genealogy/Scott-Family-Tree-52478

[38] https://www.wikitree.com/genealogy/Cavanagh-Family-Tree-1141

[39] https://www.wikitree.com/genealogy/VanLuven-Family-Tree-52

[40] https://www.wikitree.com/genealogy/Cavanagh-Family-Tree-1142

[41] https://www.wikitree.com/genealogy/Cavanagh-Family-Tree-1143

[42] https://www.wikitree.com/genealogy/Caverley-Family-Tree-53

[43] https://www.wikitree.com/genealogy/Caverley-Family-Tree-54

[44] https://www.wikitree.com/genealogy/Caverley-Family-Tree-55

[45] https://www.wikitree.com/genealogy/Horning-Family-Tree-909

[46] https://www.wikitree.com/genealogy/Caverley-Family-Tree-57

[47] https://www.wikitree.com/genealogy/Wright-Family-Tree-58232

[48] https://www.wikitree.com/genealogy/Caverly-Family-Tree-217

[49] https://www.wikitree.com/genealogy/Caverly-Family-Tree-218

[50] https://www.wikitree.com/genealogy/Bloemer-Family-Tree-15

[51] https://www.wikitree.com/genealogy/Chadwick-Family-Tree-4280

[52] https://www.wikitree.com/genealogy/Chadwick-Family-Tree-4281

Don't miss out!

Visit the website below and you can sign up to receive emails whenever Angeline Gallant publishes a new book. There's no charge and no obligation.

https://books2read.com/r/B-A-QGSI-WRRBC

BOOKS2READ

Connecting independent readers to independent writers.

Also by Angeline Gallant

Calling Her Heart
Whisper of the Heart
No Turning Back
Forsake Me Not
Hear My Cry

Keeper Of Secrets
A Lady's Secret

Midnight's Awakening
Heart of the Storm
Walking Through The Storm

Secrets of the Underworld
Deklan's Dragons

Tell My Story Collection

Tell My Story: England 1852

The Grave Whisperer
Wedding Bells in Kingston, Ontario, Canada 1923
St. Paul's Anglican Churchyard Kingston, Ontario, Canada A-B
St. Paul's Anglican Churchyard, Kingston, Ontario, Canada C - D
St. Paul's Anglican Churchyard, Kingston, Ontario, Canada G - H
St. Paul's Anglican Churchyard, Kingston, Ontario, Canada J - N
St. Paul's Anglican Churchyard, Kingston, Ontario, Canada O - R
St. Paul's Anglican Churchyard, Kingston, Ontario, Canada S - T
St. Paul's Anglican Churchyard, Kingston, Ontario T - Z
Small Graveyards & Burial Grounds: Kingston, Ontario, Canada
Cataraqui United Church Cemetery 1
Cataraqui United Church Cemetery 2

The Wolf Whisperer Series
The Cry of the Wolf
Captured Heart
Journey of the Heart
Fate's Legacy
Wolf Whisperer volumes 1 & 2
Endless White

Standalone
Winds of Change vol 1-3

Watch for more at https://www.goodreads.com/author/show/19703964.Angeline_Gallant.

www.ingramcontent.com/pod-product-compliance
Lightning Source LLC
Chambersburg PA
CBHW050607160726
48003CB00003B/1081